Oh Pray
My Wings
Are Gonna
Fit Me Well

RANDOM HOUSE   *NEW YORK*

Oh Pray
My Wings
Are Gonna
Fit Me Well

Maya Angelou

Library of Congress Cataloging in Publication Data
Angelou, Maya.
    Oh pray my wings are gonna fit me well.

    Poems.
    I. Title.
PS3551.N46405   811'.5'4   75–10268
ISBN 0–394–49951–4

    Manufactured in the United States of America

9 8 7 6 5 4

To PAUL

Contents

Part Four

Part Five

(*x*

Part One

Pickin Em Up
and Layin Em Down

There's a long-legged girl
in San Francisco
by the Golden Gate.
She said she'd give me all I wanted
but I just couldn't wait.
I started to
Pickin em up
            and layin em down,
Pickin em up
            and layin em down,
Pickin em up
            and layin em down,
gettin to the next town
Baby.

There's a pretty brown
in Birmingham
Boys, she little and cute
but when she like to tied me down
I had to grab my suit and started to
Pickin em up
            and layin em down,
Pickin em up
            and layin em down,

Pickin em up
          and layin em down,
gettin to the next town
Baby.

I met that lovely Detroit lady
and thought my time had come
But just before I said "I do"
I said "I got to run" and started to
Pickin em up
          and layin em down,
Pickin em up
          and layin em down,
Pickin em up
          and layin em down,
gettin to the next town
Baby.

There ain't no words for what I feel
about a pretty face
But if I stay I just might miss
a prettier one some place
I started to
Pickin em up
          and layin em down,
Pickin em up
          and layin em down,
Pickin em up
          and layin em down,
gettin to the next town
Baby.

Here's to Adhering

I went to a party
    out in Hollywood,
The atmosphere was shoddy
    but the drinks were good,
        and that's where I heard you laugh.

I then went cruising
    on an old Greek ship,
The crew was amusing
    but the guests weren't hip,
        that's where I found your hands.

On to the Sahara
    in a caravan,
The sun struck like an arrow
    but the nights were grand,
        and that's how I found your chest.

An evening in the Congo
    where the Congo ends,
I found myself alone, oh
    but I made some friends,
        that's where I saw your face.

I have been devoting
    all my time to get

Parts of you out floating
      still unglued as yet.

Won't you pull yourself together

For

    Me

  O N C E

On Reaching Forty

Other acquainted years
sidle
with modest
decorum
across the scrim of toughened
tears and to a stage
planked with laughter boards
and waxed with rueful loss
But forty
with the authorized
brazenness of a uniformed
cop stomps
no-knocking
into the script
bumps a funky grind on the
shabby curtain of youth
and delays the action.

Unless you have the inborn
wisdom
and grace
and are clever enough
to die at
thirty-nine.

The Telephone

It comes in black
and blue, indecisive
beige. In red and chaperons my life.
Sitting like a strict
and spinstered Aunt
spiked between my needs
and need.

It tats the day, crocheting
other people's lives
in neat arrangements
ignoring me
busy with the hemming
of strangers' overlong affairs or
the darning of my
neighbors' worn-out
dreams.

From Monday, the morning of the week,
through mid-times
noon and Sunday's dying
light. It sits silent.
Its needle sound
does not transfix my ear
or draw my longing to
a close.

Ring. Damn you!

Part Two

Passing Time

Your skin like dawn
Mine like dusk.

One paints the beginning
of a certain end.

The other, the end of a
sure beginning.

Now Long Ago

One innocent spring
your voice meant to me
less than tires turning
on a distant street.

Your name, perhaps spoken,
led no chorus of
batons
unrehearsed
to crush against my
empty chest.

That cool spring
was shortened by
your summer, bold impatient
and all forgotten
except when silence
turns the key
into my midnight bedroom
and comes to sleep upon your
pillow.

Greyday

The day hangs heavy
loose and grey
when you're away.

A crown of thorns
a shirt of hair
is what I wear.

No one knows
my lonely heart
when we're apart.

Poor Girl

You've got another love
    and I know it
Someone who adores you
    just like me
Hanging on your words
    like they were gold
Thinking that she understands
    your soul
Poor Girl
      Just like me.

You're breaking another heart
    and I know it
And there's nothing
    I can do
If I try to tell her
    what I know
She'll misunderstand
    and make me go
Poor Girl
      Just like me.

You're going to leave her too
    and I know it
She'll never know
    what made you go

She'll cry and wonder
     what went wrong
Then she'll begin
     to sing this song
Poor Girl
     Just like me.

Come. And Be My Baby

The highway is full of big cars
going nowhere fast
And folks is smoking anything that'll burn
Some people wrap their lives around a cocktail glass
And you sit wondering
where you're going to turn
I got it.
Come. And be my baby.

Some prophets say the world is gonna end tomorrow
But others say we've got a week or two
The paper is full of every kind of blooming horror
And you sit wondering
What you're gonna do.
I got it.
Come. And be my baby.

Senses of Insecurity

I couldn't tell fact from fiction
    or if my dream was true,
The only sure prediction
    in this whole world was you.
I'd touched your features inchly
    heard love and dared the cost.
The scented spiel reeled me unreal
    and found my senses lost.

Alone

Lying, thinking
Last night
How to find my soul a home
Where water is not thirsty
And bread loaf is not stone
I came up with one thing
And I don't believe I'm wrong
That nobody,
But nobody
Can make it out here alone.

Alone, all alone
Nobody, but nobody
Can make it out here alone.

There are some millionaires
With money they can't use
Their wives run round like banshees
Their children sing the blues
They've got expensive doctors
To cure their hearts of stone.
But nobody
No nobody
Can make it out here alone.

Alone, all alone
Nobody, but nobody
Can make it out here alone.

Now if you listen closely
I'll tell you what I know
Storm clouds are gathering
The wind is gonna blow
The race of man is suffering
And I can hear the moan,
Cause nobody,
But nobody
Can make it out here alone.

Alone, all alone
Nobody, but nobody
Can make it out here alone.

Communication I

She wished of him a lover's kiss and
nights of coupled twining
They laced themselves
between the trees
and to the water's edge.

Reminding her
the cratered moon lay light years away
he spoke of Greece, the Parthenon
and Cleopatra's barge.

She splayed her foot
up to the shin
within the ocean brine.

He quoted Pope and Bernard Shaw
and Catcher in the Rye.

Her sandal lost
she dried her toe
and then she mopped her brow.

Dry-eyed
she walked into her room
and frankly told her mother
"Of all he said I understood,
he said he loved another."

For Adele

Communication II

The Student

The dust of ancient pages
had never touched his face,
and fountains black and comely
were mummyied in a place
beyond
his young un-knowing.

The Teacher

She shared the lettered strivings
of etched Pharaonic walls
and Reconstruction's anguish
resounded down the halls
of all her
dry dreams.

Wonder

A day
drunk with the nectar of
nowness
weaves its way between
the years
to find itself at the flophouse
of night
to sleep and be seen
no more.

Will I be less
dead because I wrote this
poem or you more because
you read it
long years hence.

A Conceit

Give me your hand

Make room for me
to lead and follow
you
beyond this rage of poetry.

Let others have
the privacy of
touching words
and love of loss
of love.

For me
Give me your hand.

Part Three

Request

If this country is a bastard
will the lowdown mother user
who ran off
and left the woman
moaning in her
green delivery
please come back and claim
his love child.
Give a legal name to beg from
for the first
time of its life.

Africa

Thus she had lain
sugar cane sweet
deserts her hair
golden her feet
mountains her breasts
two Niles her tears
Thus she has lain
Black through the years.

Over the white seas
rime white and cold
brigands ungentled
icicle bold
took her young daughters
sold her strong sons
churched her with Jesus
bled her with guns.
Thus she has lain.

Now she is rising
remember her pain
remember the losses
her screams loud and vain
remember her riches
her history slain
now she is striding
although she had lain.

America

The gold of her promise
    has never been mined

Her borders of justice
    not clearly defined

Her crops of abundance
    the fruit and the grain

Have not fed the hungry
    nor eased that deep pain

Her proud declarations
    are leaves on the wind

Her southern exposure
    black death did befriend

Discover this country
    dead centuries cry

Erect noble tablets
    where none can decry

"She kills her bright future
    and rapes for a sou

Then entraps her children
        with legends untrue"

I beg you

Discover this country.

For Us, Who Dare Not Dare

Be me a Pharaoh
Build me high pyramids of stone and question
See me the Nile
at twilight
and jaguars moving to
the slow cool draught.

Swim me Congo
Hear me the tails of alligators
flapping waves that reach
a yester shore.

Swing me vines, beyond that Bao-Bab tree,
and talk me chief
Sing me birds
flash color lightening through bright green leaves.

Taste me fruit
its juice free falling from
a mother tree.

Know me

Africa.

for Countee Cullen

Lord, In My Heart

Holy haloes
    Ring me round

Spirit waves on
    Spirit sound

Meshach and
    Abednego

Golden chariot
    Swinging low

I recite them
    in my sleep

Jordan's cold
    and briny deep

Bible lessons
    Sunday school

Bow before the
    Golden Rule

Now I wonder
If I tried

Could I turn my
cheek aside

Marvelling with
afterthought

Let the blow fall
saying naught

Of my true Christ-
like control

and the nature
of my soul.

Would I strike with
rage divine

Till the culprit
fell supine

Hit out broad all
fury red

Till my foes are
fallen dead

Teachers of my
    early youth

Taught forgiveness
    stressed the truth

Here then is my
    Christian lack:

If I'm struck then
    I'll strike back.

Artful Pose

Of falling leaves and melting
snows, of birds
in their delights
Some poets sing
their melodies
tendering my nights
sweetly.

My pencil halts
and will not go
along that quiet path
I need to write
of lovers false

and hate
and hateful wrath
quickly.

Part Four

The Couple

Discard the fear and what
was she?   of rag and bones
a mimicry of woman's
fairy ness
Archaic at its birth

Discharge the hate and when
was he?   disheveled moans
a mimesis of man's
estate
deceited for its worth

Dissolve the greed and why
were they?   enfeebled thrones
a memory of mortal
kindliness
exiled from this earth.

The Pusher

He bad
O he bad
He make a honky
poot. Make a honky's
blue eyes squint
anus tight, when
my man look in
the light blue eyes.

He thinks
He don't play
His Afro crown raises
eyes. Raises eyebrows
of wonder and dark
envy when he, combed
out, hits the street.

He sleek
Dashiki
Wax printed on his skin
remembrances of Congo dawns
laced across his chest.
Red Blood Red and Black.

He bought
O He got

Malcolm's paper
back. Checked out the
photo, caught a few godly
lines. Then wondered how
many wives/daughters of
Honky (miscalled The Man)
bird snake
caught, dug them both.
(Him, Fro-ed Dashiki-ed
and the book.)

He stashed
He stands stashed
Near, too near the MLK
Library. P.S. naught
naught naught. Breathing
slaughter on the Malcolm X
Institute. Whole fist
balled, fingers pressing
palm. Shooting up through
Honky's blue-eyed sky.

      "BLACK IS!"
      "NATION TIME!"
      "TOMORROW'S GLORY HERE TODAY"

Pry free the hand
Observe our Black present.
There lie soft on that
copper palm, a death of

coke. A kill of horse
eternal night's barbiturates.
One hundred youths
sped down to
Speed.

He right
O he bad
He badder than death
yet gives no sweet
release.

Chicken-Licken

She was afraid of men,
sin and the humors
of the night.
When she saw a bed
locks clicked
in her brain.

She screwed a frown
around and plugged
it in the keyhole.
Put a chain across
her door and closed
her mind.

Her bones were found
round thirty years later
when they razed
her building to
put up a parking lot.

Autopsy: read
dead of acute peoplelessness.

Part Five

I Almost Remember

I almost remember
    smiling some
years past
    even combing the ceiling
with the teeth of a laugh
(longer ago than the
        smile).
Open night news-eyed I watch
channels of hunger
    written on children's faces
    bursting bellies balloon
in the air of my day room.

There was a smile, I recall
now jelled in
a never yester glow. Even a laugh
that tickled the tits of
heaven
(older than the smile).
In graphs, afraid, I see the black
brown hands and
white thin yellowed fingers.

Slip slipping from the
ledge of life. Forgotten by
all but hatred.

Ignored
by all but disdain.

On late evenings when
quiet inhabits my garden
when grass sleeps and
streets are only paths for silent
mist.

I seem to remember

Smiling.

Prisoner

Even sunlight dares
and trembles through
my bars
to shimmer
dances on
the floor.
A clang of
lock and
keys and heels
and blood-dried
guns.
Even sunshine
dares.

It's jail
          and bail
then rails to run.

Guard grey men
serve plates of rattle
noise and concrete
death and beans
Then pale sun stumbles
through the poles of
iron to warm the horror
of grey guard men.

It's jail
        and bail
then rails to run.

Black night. The me
myself of me sleeks
in the folds and history
of fear. To secret hold
me deep and close my
ears of lulls and clangs
and memory of hate.
Then night and sleep
and dreams.

It's jail
        and bail
then rails to run.

Woman Me

Your smile, delicate
rumor of peace.
Deafening revolutions nestle in the
cleavage of
your breasts
Beggar-Kings and red-ringed Priests
seek glory at the meeting
of your thighs
A grasp of Lions,   A lap of Lambs.

Your tears, jeweled
strewn a diadem
caused Pharaohs to ride
deep in the bosom of the
Nile. Southern spas lash fast
their doors upon the night when
winds of death blow down your name
A bride of hurricanes,   A swarm of summer wind.

Your laughter, pealing tall
above the bells of ruined cathedrals.
Children reach between your teeth
for charts to live their lives.
A stomp of feet,   A bevy of swift hands.

John J.

His soul curdled
standing milk
      childhood's right gone wrong.

Plum blue, skin brown dusted
eyes black shining,
      (His momma didn't want him)

The round head slick silk
Turn around, fall down curls
Old ladies smelling of flour
and talcum powder Cashmere Bouquet, said
"This child is pretty enough to be a girl."
      (But his momma didn't want him)

John J. grinned a "How can you resist me?"
and danced to conjure lightning from
a morning's summer sky.
Gave the teacher an apple kiss
      (But his momma didn't want him)

His nerves stretched two thousand miles
found a flinging singing lady,
breasting a bar
calling straights on the dice,
gin over ice,

and the 30's version of
everybody in the
pool.

(She didn't want him.)

Southeast Arkanasia

After Eli Whitney's gin
brought to generations' end
bartered flesh and broken bones
Did it cleanse you of your sin
    Did you ponder?

Now, when farmers bury wheat
and the cow men dump the sweet
butter down on Davy Jones
Does it sanctify your street
    Do you wonder?

Or is guilt your nightly mare
bucking wake your evenings' share
of the stilled repair of groans
and the absence of despair
    over yonder?

Song for the Old Ones

My Fathers sit on benches
  their flesh count every plank
  the slats leave dents of darkness
deep in their withered flanks.

They nod like broken candles
  all waxed and burnt profound,
  they say "It's understanding
that makes the world go round."

There in those pleated faces
  I see the auction block
  the chains and slavery's coffles
the whip and lash and stock.

My Fathers speak in voices
  that shred my fact and sound
  they say "It's our submission
that makes the world go round."

They used the finest cunning
  their naked wits and wiles
  the lowly Uncle Tomming
and Aunt Jemimas' smiles.

They've laughed to shield their crying
        then shuffled through their dreams
        and stepped 'n fetched a country
to write the blues with screams.

I understand their meaning
        it could and did derive
        from living on the edge of death
They kept my race alive.

Child Dead in Old Seas

Father,
I wait for you in oceans
tides washing pyramids high
above my head.
Waves, undulating
corn rows around my
black feet.
The heavens shift and
stars find holes set
new in dark infirmity.
My search goes on.
Dainty shells on ash-like wrists
of debutantes remember you.
Childhood's absence has
not stilled your
voice. My ear
listens. You whisper
on the watery passage.

Deep dirges moan
from the
belly of the sea
and your song
floats to me
of lost savannahs
green and

drums. Of palm trees bending
woman-like swaying
grape-blue children
laugh on beaches
of sand as
white as your bones
clean
on the foot of
long-ago waters.

Father.
I wait for you
wrapped in
the entrails of
whales. Your
blood now
blues
spume
over
the rippled
surface of our
grave.

Take Time Out

When you see them
on a freeway hitching rides
wearing beads
with packs by their sides
you ought to ask
What's all the
warring and the jarring
and the
killing and
the thrilling
all about.

Take Time Out.

When you see him
with a band around his head
and an army surplus bunk
that makes his bed. You'd
better ask What's
all the
beating and
the cheating and
the bleeding and
the needing
all about.

Take Time Out.

When you see her walking
Barefoot in the rain
And you know she's tripping
on a one-way train
you need to ask
what's all the
lying and the
dying and
the running and
the gunning
all about.

Take Time Out.

Use a minute
feel some sorrow
for the folks
who think tomorrow
is a place that they
can call up
on the phone.
Take a month
and show some kindness
for the folks
who thought that blindness
was an illness that
affected eyes alone.

If you know that youth
is dying on the run

and my daughter trades
dope stories with your son
we'd better see
what all our
fearing and our
jeering and our
crying and
our lying
brought about.

Take Time Out.

for Harriet Tubman & Fredrick Douglass

Elegy

I lay down in my grave
and watch my children
grow
Proud blooms
above the weeds of death.

Their petals wave
and still nobody
knows the soft black
dirt that is my winding
sheet. The worms, my friends,
yet tunnel holes in
bones and through those
apertures I see the rain.
The sunfelt warmth
now jabs
within my space and
brings me roots of my
children born.

Their seeds must fall
and press beneath
this earth,
and find me where I

wait. My only need to
fertilize their birth.

I lay down in my grave
and watch my children
grow.

Reverses

How often must we
   butt to head
Mind to ass
   flank to nuts
   cock to elbow
   hip to toe
   soul to shoulder
   confront ourselves
   in our past.

Little Girl Speakings

Ain't nobody better's my Daddy,
    you keep yo' quauter
    I ain't yo' daughter,
Ain't nobody better's my Daddy.

Ain't nothing prettier'n my dollie
    heard what I said,
    don't pat her head,
Ain't nothing prettier'n my dollie.

No lady cookinger than my Mommy
    smell that pie,
    see I don't lie
No lady cookinger than my Mommy.

This Winter Day

The kitchen is its readiness
white green and orange things
leak their blood selves in the soup.

Ritual sacrifice that snaps
an odor at my nose and starts
my tongue to march
slipping in the liquid of it drip.

The day, silver striped
in rain, is balked against
my window and the soup.

About the Author

MAYA ANGELOU is the author of the best-selling *I Know Why the Caged Bird Sings, Gather Together in My Name,* and another poetry collection, *Just Give Me a Cool Drink of Water 'fore I Diiie.* She has studied dance in San Francisco, has toured Europe and Africa for the State Department in *Porgy and Bess,* and has taught dance in Rome and Tel Aviv. In collaboration with Godfrey Cambridge, Ms. Angelou produced, directed, and starred in *Cabaret for Freedom* at the Village Gate. She starred in Genet's *The Blacks* at the St. Mark's Playhouse and at the request of the late Martin Luther King, Jr., became the Northern Coordinator for the Southern Christian Leadership Conference. During a stay in Africa, Ms. Angelou was on the faculty of the University of Ghana and wrote for newspapers in Cairo and in Ghana. Her other credits include: writer and producer of a ten-part TV series on African traditions in American life, original screenwriter and composer for the film *Georgia, Georgia,* adapter of Sophocles' *Ajax* for the Mark Taper Forum in Los Angeles, and guest interviewer for the PBS program *Assignment America.* She is also the director of the television feature films *Tapestry* and *Circles.*

Maya Angelou lives in Sonoma, California.